THE ADVENTURES OF GRACIE & MONKEYBEAR

Book 2: Winter

C. S. O'KELLY

illustrator Jordy Farrell

NEPAL

AIRSHIPS

"Monkey Bear," Gracie whispered. "Something was in the backyard last night."

"RRR... RRUFF?" asked a super-sleepy MonkeyBear.

"It couldn't have been Grandma's dog, silly. YOU were asleep."

"ROOF." He yawned and reached for his red scarf.

"Aaa... aaa... aaa..." echoed from the corner of the yard.

"It's a cry for help, MonkeyBear. For all the girls in all the worlds!" Gracie shouted.

And like every Saturday before, just as the sun touched her backyard, Gracie and MonkeyBear were off on their latest adventure.

"ROOF ROOF."

"Where, MonkeyBear? Wait... there."

A shadow appeared, then vanished.

"Aaa..." sounded deep from the tunnel.

"It's a Yeti! And his yak is stuck."

"Don't worry, Yeshe Yeti, MonkeyBear and I will help Yomo Yak."

"ROOF."

"We could use our ice tools?"

"RARF ROO ROO," suggested MonkeyBear.

"Even better. I'll get them." Gracie raced out of the cave toward Grandma's house.

A puddle appeared... and quickly grew.

"Aaa..." Part of Yomo Yak's tongue came free of the ice.
"Aaaa..." Only a small piece remained stuck.
"Aaaaa..." POP! Yomo Yak was free.

"Look out!" Gracie ran in. "The ice is splitting, jump, MonkeyBear!"

CRACK! CRACK! SNAP! ...a rushing sound filled the cave.

"A boat like this could work and I brought our ice tools."

"ROOF," MonkeyBear agreed, and Yeshe Yeti's table was just the right size with plenty of room for snacks.

"That's perfect for a sail, Yeshe Yeti!" Gracie said. "Thank you."

MonkeyBear kept an eye on Yomo Yak, who wanted to lick the ice just one more time.

"Bye, Yeshe Yeti! So long, Yomo Yak!"

Gracie steered, and a powerful wind filled their sail, pushing them into a swirling storm.

From far atop the mountain peak, something fluffy?

Something furry? Something with a tail!

Rolled, bounced, and tumbled toward them.

Eyes appeared in the furry pile of snow. "Puff, hissss, hissss mew."

"What did she say, MonkeyBear?"

"RUFF RUFF GROOF, RO RO ROOF," he explained.

"Sashi Snow Leopard... and you're stuck. We'll get you home."

"This airship is our best design ever, MonkeyBear!"

"Purrrr purrrr poof," Sashi Snow Leopard agreed.

"We have liftoff!" Gracie shouted above the howling winds. "MonkeyBear, tell Sashi Snow Leopard to steer toward her den... and hold on!"

"GROO ROO ROOF!" MonkeyBear barked, and Sashi Snow Leopard dug in her claws and grabbed the pilot's wheel.

"WOOF WOOF!"

"I know we need more power, MonkeyBear!" a tired Gracie answered. "Crank faster!"

Suddenly the whirling, whistling wind was gone...

The airship burst through the dark clouds and into sunlight.

Gracie and MonkeyBear waved goodbye to Sashi Snow Leopard. Below their airship, the clouds turned black and thunder rattled and roared.

"ROOF ROO RO," said a worried MonkeyBear.

"We can go higher and find a way around the storm," Gracie said.

Lightning flashed, thunder boomed, and a dark shadow appeared.

"RRROOO RRROOO..."

"I'm scared too, MonkeyBear, but we need to go higher."

"RO ROO."

"I love you too! Our airship is strong and so are we!" said Gracie.

"ROOF!" roared MonkeyBear, and he cranked the propeller as fast as he could.

"Well, at least we're above the storm."

Gracie looked into the biggest eyes she had ever seen.

"It's a spirit-animal," she whispered, "a Thunder Dragon. Finally, MonkeyBear, I get to speak Dzongkha."

"ང་བདེན་པ་འབྲུག་ཡིན། འདི་ཡིན་ཏྲོ་ཅན་གྱིས་སྐྱག་འདི་གིས། དེ་གི་མིག་འཕུལ་གྱི་ནར་ཐ་ཐའི་འབབ་ ཡར་སེ། ད་ ང་རང་འཕུར་མི་ཚུགས་པས། [I am Denpa Druk. This angry cloud took my magic stripes and I can no longer fly]."

"མོང་གི་བི་ཡར་དང་ང་གིས་ཚ་རོགས་འབད་ཚུགས། ང་བ་ཅས་ཚ་གིས་གནམ་ལུ་ བསྐྱར་བཙེས་དགོ པ་ཅིག་ཆུན་དགོ [MonkeyBear and I can help! We just need to make a

"It's working! But our airship is melting!"

"GROOF GROOO ROOOOF!"

MonkeyBear spotted the perfect landing place through a hole in the clouds.

"བདེན་པ་འབྲུག ཨ་ཙེ་ཚིག་སློག [Hold on, Denpa Druk]!"

"གོ་རེ་སི་དང་མོང་ཀི་བི་ཡར་གཉིས་ལུ། བཀྲིན་ཆེ་ཟེར་ལུ་ནི། [Thank you, Gracie and MonkeyBear]."

"བདེན་པ་འབྲུག་ལ་ཚ་ཅིག་ཡར་སྐྱག་ལུ། བཅུབ་བས། [You're welcome, and your magic stripes are beautiful]!"

...the airship was melting in the sunshine, but MonkeyBear had

"བདེན་པ་འབྲུག །ཨ་ཚ་ཅིག་ཡར་ལྡག་ལ། བཅུབ་ཐས། [Just a little bit higher, Denpa Druk, perfect]."

"ROOF, RUFF ROOROO!" echoed MonkeyBear.

"I know it's melting. I'm working as fast as I can–"

The wind carried a familiar voice from far away.

"Gracie...

"MonkeyBear..."

It was time to leave. They waved goodbye to Denpa Druk.

"Prepare for launch, MonkeyBear!" Gracie began the countdown.

"གསུམ [Three]...
"གཉིས [Two]...
"གཅིག [One]...
"འགྲོ་བཙུགས། [Launch]!"

And Denpa Druk let go...

Grandma's loving voice grew louder with each icy turn.

"Gracie...

"MonkeyBear..."

And like every Saturday before, just as the sun disappeared behind their house, Gracie and MonkeyBear were back from their latest adventure and ready for dinner.

Published by MonkeyBear Publishing
An imprint of Lore Mountain Productions
www.loremountain.com

The Adventures of Gracie & MonkeyBear, Gracie & MonkeyBear, MonkeyBear Publishing, and the MonkeyBear name and logo are registered trademarks of Lore Mountain Productions. The publisher is not responsible for websites (or their content) that are not owned by the publisher.

First Edition: November 2017
Library of Congress Control Number: 2017951943 · ISBN 978-1-946807-02-1
Manufactured in the USA · Printed on acid free paper

Special thanks to illustrator Jordy Farrell, editor Tricia Callahan, designer Arial Light, and Dzongkha translation by World Translation Center. As with all great things, it takes a team to see it through. These incredibly talented and wonderful people enabled the author to take his story and vision and craft it into The Adventures of Gracie & MonkeyBear. Without them, it would not exist.

for Cadán

Publisher's Cataloging-In-Publication Data
(Prepared by The Donohue Group, Inc.)

Names: O'Kelly, C. S. | Farrell, Jordy, illustrator.
Title: The adventures of Gracie & MonkeyBear / C.S. O'Kelly ; illustrator, Jordy Farrell.
Other Titles: Adventures of Gracie and MonkeyBear
Description: First edition. | [Lower Lake, California] : MonkeyBear Publishing, an imprint of Lore Mountain
    Productions, 2017. | Interest age level: 005-009. | Contents: Book 2: Winter. | Summary: "From their
    backyard in Brooklyn, Gracie & MonkeyBear find portals to new worlds. With each new doorway comes the
    opportunity to help those in need and create lasting friendships along the way. Gracie and MonkeyBear are
    tested at every turn ... But can they make it home in time for dinner?"--Provided by publisher.
Identifiers: ISBN 9781946807021 (Book 2: hardcover) | ISBN 9781946807038 (Book 2: ebook)
Subjects: LCSH: Explorers--Juvenile fiction. | Girls--Juvenile fiction. | Dogs--Juvenile fiction. | Friendship-
    -Juvenile fiction. | Seasons--Juvenile fiction. | CYAC: Explorers--Fiction. | Girls--Fiction. | Dogs--Fiction. |
    Friendship--Fiction. | Seasons--Fiction. | LCGFT: Action and adventure fiction.
Classification: LCC PZ7.1.O445 Ad 2017 (print) | LCC PZ7.1.O445 (ebook) | DDC [E]--dc23

CPSIA information can be obtained
at www.ICGtesting.com
Printed in the USA
LVHW01n1741120218
566241LV00012B/193/P